400
PICTURE
WRITING
PROMPTS

Visual Story Starters
to Spark Creativity

BY HUDSON CREATIVE WORKS

scribe
& dot
BOOKS

If you find this book helpful, please consider leaving a rating and comment for it where you purchased it, or on Amazon. We'd love to know how you used it, what you were inspired to write, what worked for you, and what did not. Your feedback helps us improve and create more books like it.

Thank you,

HUDSON CREATIVE WORKS

INTRODUCTION

Hello, and thank you for choosing *400 Picture Writing Prompts* for your creative writing inspiration! We're delighted for the opportunity to share with you what we believe—that images can be powerful catalysts for writing.

As you may have gathered, this book is a bit different from other writing prompt books. We're writers and designers, which means our craft is communicating through words and images. But human brains are wired for visual information and process images 60,000 times faster than text, and you don't need to be a writer or a designer to understand the power of images to spark ideas. It comes naturally, which is why images are such an effective creative tool.

Another thing we'd like to note is that not all images are of the same quality; there's a lot of flotsam out there, to be frank. You won't find, "businessman gesturing to a whiteboard," or "woman feigning surprise in front of a generic photo backdrop," here. That may be suitable for a business presentation, but our image prompts have been carefully curated with the writer in mind and a designer's editorial eye.

When we created this workbook, we searched through thousands of images to find ones that represented a variety of experiences, were full of storytelling possibilities, and could work across genres. Each image in this book has been hand-selected both for its aesthetic and narrative value.

The exercises themselves don't require much in the way of commitment. Just dive in and don't worry about making things perfect. The picture should do the heavy lifting, help you ideate, stretch your creative muscles, get limber, and flow. Please give your inner critic the day off.

There are innumerable ways you can use the prompts and no right or wrong ways to do it. We've provided a few ideas to help build characters, scenes, plots, and dialogue. We've also offered some suggestions for different approaches to get more out of your prompts.

Whether you write novels, short stories, poems, plays, scripts, or blog posts, we hope these prompts will help facilitate your creative process. Not only can individual writers benefit from picture prompts, but they're great for classes, writing groups, and workshops as well.

There are extra lined pages at the end should you need the space, but it may help to keep another notebook on hand for your scribblings if you're more prolific than that—and we hope you are!

We'd be thrilled if any of these prompts inspire you to write. If you care to share feedback by leaving a comment where you purchased the book, or on Amazon, we'd love that too.

Let's get writing!

HUDSON CREATIVE WORKS

STORY ELEMENTS

Characters, settings, plots, and dialogue are the basic building blocks of a story. If you need somewhere to start with your prompt, try asking any of the following questions, or a combination, to get the ball rolling.

Character

1. Describe what the character looks like.
2. How old are they?
3. What are they doing?
4. What are they wearing?
5. What is their demeanor?
6. What is their expression?
7. What are their mannerisms?
8. How are they feeling?
9. What are they thinking?
10. What is their personality like?
11. What are their motivations?
12. What makes them unusual, unique, or interesting?
13. Where do they live?
14. How do they speak? Do they speak?
15. What does their voice sound like?
16. What do they like? Dislike?
17. Do they have dreams and aspirations?

Setting

1. Describe the setting.
2. Where does it take place?
3. Is it interior, urban, suburban, rural, extraterrestrial, multidimensional?
4. What are some adjectives to describe it?
5. What type of vegetation grows there?
6. What type of animals live there?
7. Do people live there? How many? What kind?
8. Are there any buildings or structures?
9. What materials were used to build it?
10. What is the history of this place?
11. What time of day is it?
12. What time of year?
13. What is the climate like?
14. What is the air like?
15. What are the smells?
16. What are the colors of this place?

Plot / Action

1. Describe what is happening.
2. What, if any, action is going on here?
3. When is it happening?
4. Where is it happening?
5. What happened before this moment?
6. What happens afterward?
7. Is this part of the main plot? Or a subplot?
8. Is there conflict?
9. Is there resolution?

Dialogue

1. Describe the dialogue.
2. Who is speaking? How many people?
3. What are they saying?
4. Describe the nature of the interaction. Are they happy, sad, calm, spirited, angry, argumentative, demanding, suspicious?
5. What other forms of communication, perhaps unspoken, are there? Are they gesturing, making expressions?

EXERCISES

These exercises help you get more out of your visual prompts. Give yourself limitations, look at it through a different lens, leave it to chance, add a twist, change an aspect of the prompt itself, or two or three.

Choose an image

You can go from 1 to 400 sequentially, or simply select an image you like. You can also close your eyes, flip through the book, open it to a random page, and point. The prompt that is closest, is your prompt. Whichever method you chose, please look at the image and then write 5 things about it.

Choose multiple images

You don't need to limit yourself to just one image. Try selecting two or more and turning those into a narrative. How are they related? How would you tie them together? Do the storylines intersect? Are they happening sequentially? Simultaneously? In what order do they happen? Now you have the start of a plot.

Randomize words and images

This is the same exercise as using multiple images, only instead of choosing them yourself, you leave it to chance. To do this, you can go to a website like random.org. Set the minimum parameter to 1, and the maximum to 400. Generate two or more numbers—say, 6, 18, and 204—then use those images as your prompts. You can also use the same site, or any other method you like, to generate random words.

Change the details

Perhaps you find some parts of an image useful—an expression on someone's face, a small detail off to the side—but not others. Or maybe you want to challenge yourself. Change any aspect of an image if it suits you—gender, ethnicity, location, subject, perspective, emotion, etc., are all up for grabs.

Where are we?

Where does the image occur in your story—the beginning, middle, or end? How about an epilogue? What happens if you switch the order in which the events take place?

Start in the middle

Have you ever read a story or seen a film that begins in the middle? This narrative technique is called *in medias res*, which is Latin for "in the midst of things."

Take a classic comedy film trope which opens in the middle of a chaotic scene. You see the character in a situation that becomes increasingly absurd. At the height of the insanity you hear a record scratch. The image freezes and a voice over narrator says, "You may wonder how I got here...", then the story flashes back to an earlier point in time.

Limit yourself to 5, 10, or 15 minutes, and write an opening with your prompt that starts in the middle of the action.

Add a twist

You're going to turn an image on its head. Not literally, although you could do that too. There are drawing exercises that have you do just that; draw an image while looking at it upside-down and the results may surprise you.

What if something is not as it appears? What if *nothing* is as it seems? What if what you see doesn't even exist? What if the monster is the hero? The underdog is the villain? The future is the past?

Another way to flip the script is to change the scale or perspective. You can experiment with broadening and narrowing the context. Is one storyline part of a much larger epic? Or is the action happening on a very small scale, like in a snow globe, or a person's mind?

Introduce variables and conflict

Begin with an image, character, or scene. Now, introduce a variable into the equation. What happens if you take an idyllic image of a farm and add... a couple arguing? A drought? A tornado? A UFO?

An example of this would be the iconic scene from the Alfred Hitchcock film, *North by Northwest*, where the main character, played by Cary Grant, is dropped off on a lonely stretch of road next to a cornfield. At first, nothing much happens. He idly observes a crop duster flying in the distance, but boredom soon gives way to tension as the plane turns and begins flying towards him. What happens next is a masterful construction of mystery and suspense without even any dialogue.

Experiment with genres

What happens to an image when you look at it through the lens of a different genre? If it's a romance, does it change? How does it work as a scene from fantasy? What about a detective story? Try to apply one of the following genres to your visual prompt. You can also mix genres. If you don't see a category, you can add it to the spaces below.

Comedy ....
Children ....
Drama ....
Historical ....
Horror ....
Mystery / Thriller ....
Romance ....
Satire ....
Sci-Fi / Fantasy ....
Historical ....
Young Adult ....
Western ....

Even if you primarily engage in other forms of writing—literary fiction, poetry, nonfiction, essays, criticism, etc.—you can still try the exercise, if you like. It's simply a way to look at something from a different perspective. It might even be fun and instructive for you to write in a style you're not accustomed to. You might discover you have a knack for it and enjoy it! And if you're already into a particular genre, you may consider using the prompts to generate ideas and expand into different areas as well.

WRITE YOUR OWN EXERCISES

Are there other exercises and techniques you can think of? Jot them down on this page, along with any other ideas.

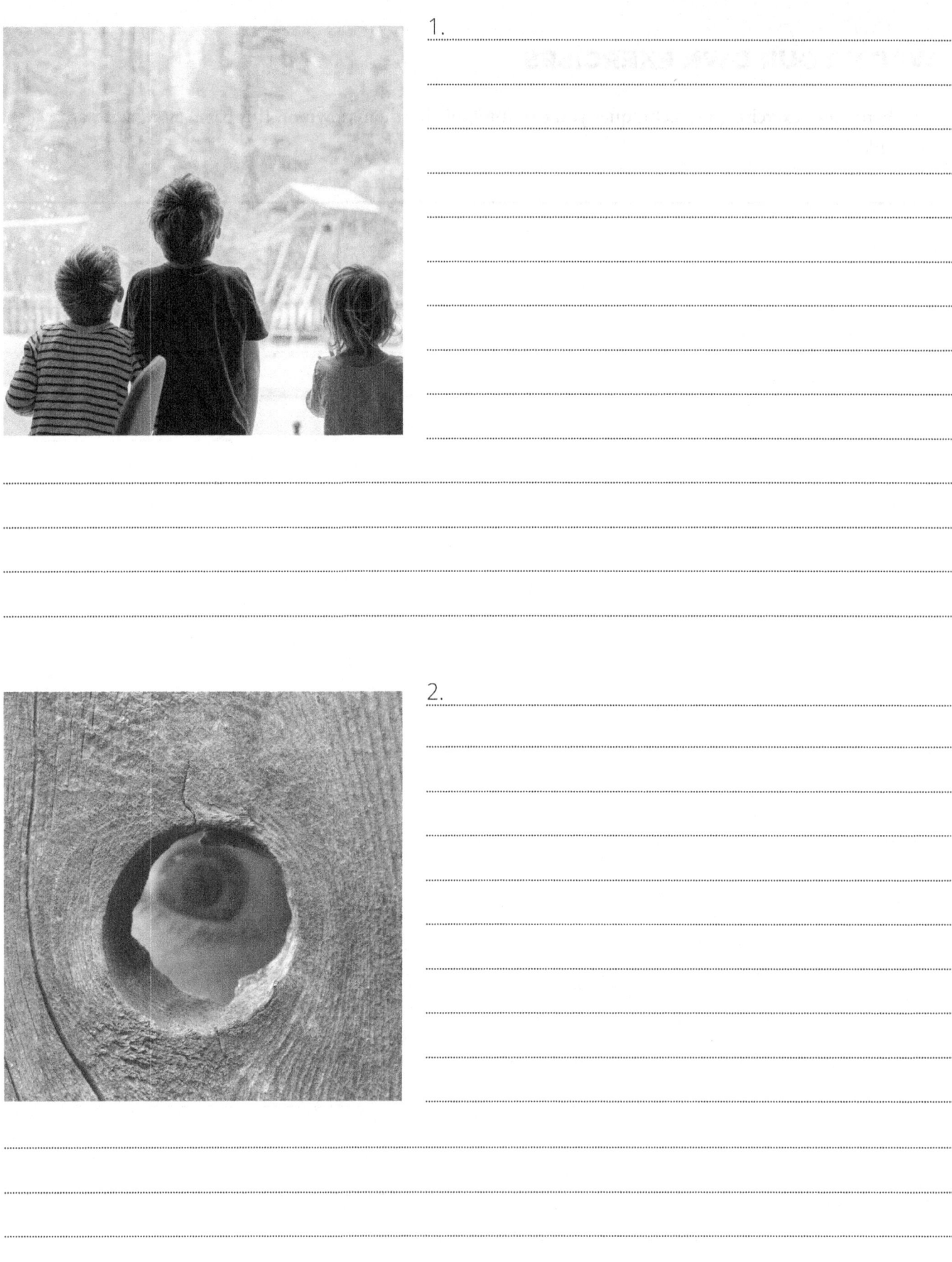

1.

2.

3.

....
....
....
....
....
....
....
....
....
....
....

4.

....
....
....
....
....
....
....
....
....
....
....

5. ....
....
....
....
....
....
....
....
....
....
....

6. ....
....
....
....
....
....
....
....
....
....
....
....

7.
....
....
....
....
....
....
....
....
....
....
....
....
....

8.
....
....
....
....
....
....
....
....
....
....
....
....
....

9.

10.

11.

12.

13.

14.

15.

16.

17.

18.

19.

20.

21.
....
....
....
....
....
....
....
....
....
....
....
....

22.
....
....
....
....
....
....
....
....
....
....
....
....

23.

24.

25.

26.

27.

28.

29.

30.

31.

32.

33.

34.

24

35.

36.

Venice, Italy

37.

38.

39.

40.

41.
....
....
....
....
....
....
....
....
....
....
....
....

42.
....
....
....
....
....
....
....
....
....
....
....
....
....

43.

44.

45.

Paris, France

46.

30

47.

48.

49.

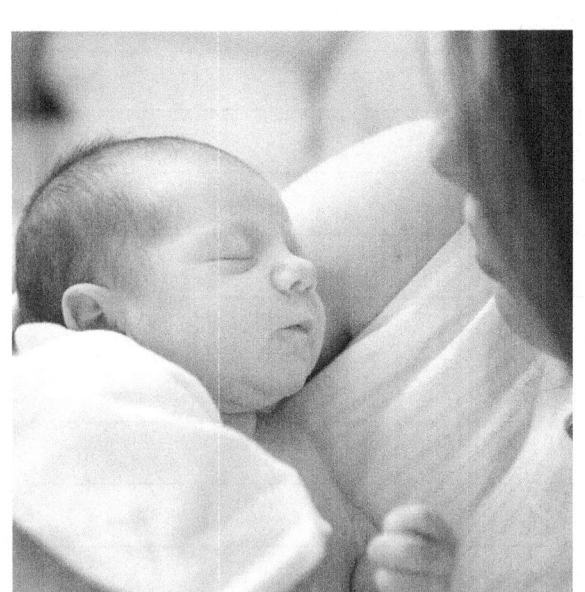

50.

32

51.

52.

53.

54.

55.

London, England

56.

57.

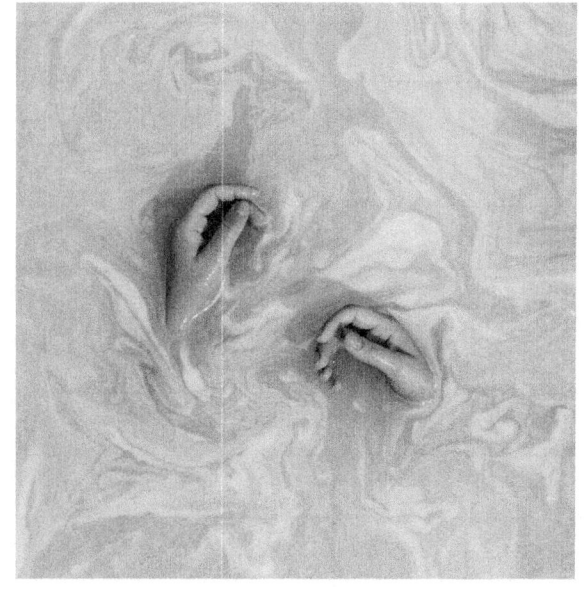

58.

59.

60.

61.

62.

63.

64.

65.

66.

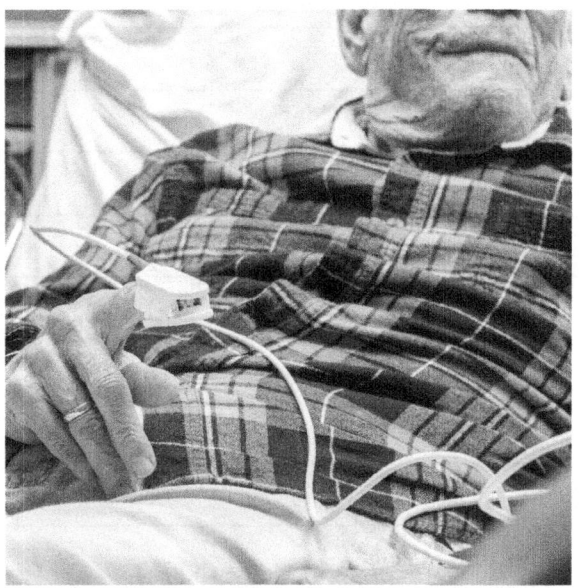

67.

68.

69.

70.

71.

72.

43

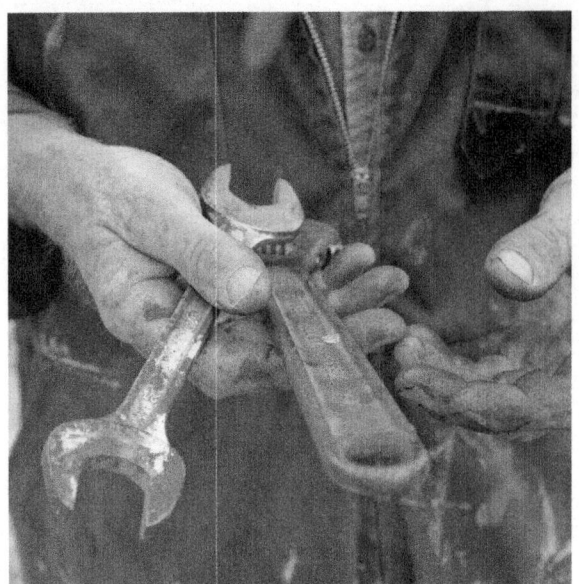

73.

74.

75.

76.

77.

78.

46

79.

80.

81.

82.

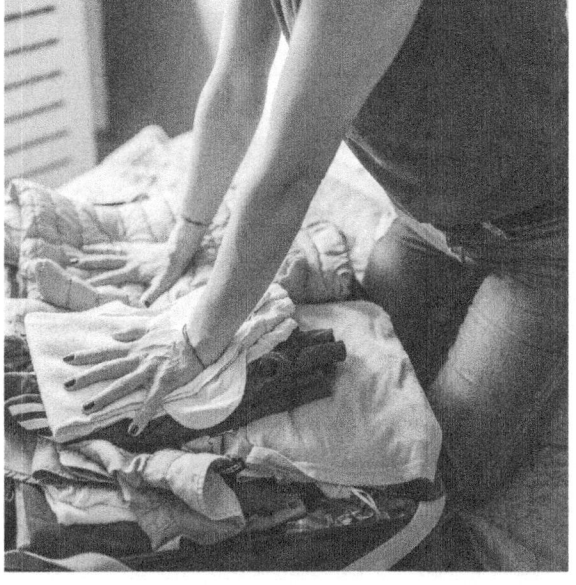

83.

84.

85.

86.

87.

88.

51

89.

90.

91.

92.

93.

94.

95.

96.

97.

98.

99.

100.

101.

102.

County Limerick, Ireland

103.

104.

Methoni, Greece

105.

106.

107.

108.

Cape Town, South Africa

109.

110.

111.

112.

Easter Island, Chile

113.

114.

115.

116.

117.

118.

119.

120.

121.

122.

123.

124.

125.

126.

127.

128.

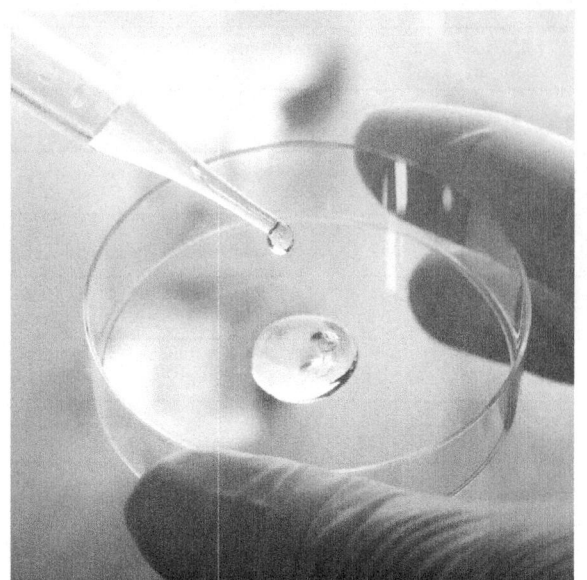

129.

130.

Paro, Bhutan

131.

132.

Paro, Bhutan

133.

134.

135.

136.

137.

138.

76

Chiang Mai, Thailand

139.

140.

141.

142.

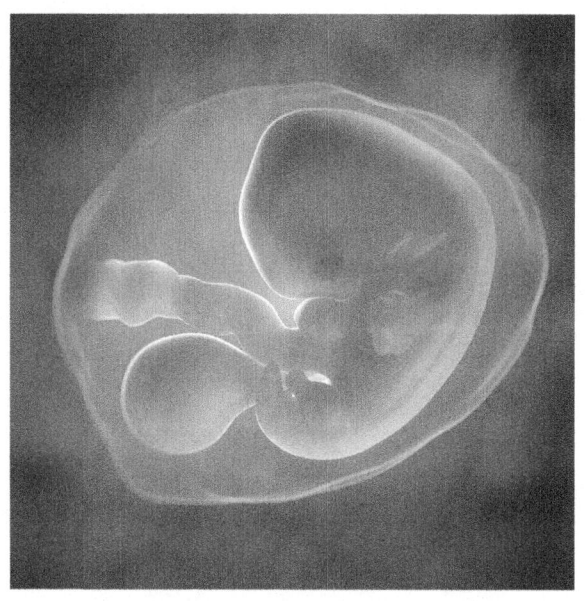

143.

Rio de Janeiro, Brazil

144.

145.

146.

Sine-Saloum, Senegal

147.

148.

#.

149.

#

150.

151.

152.

153.

154.

155.

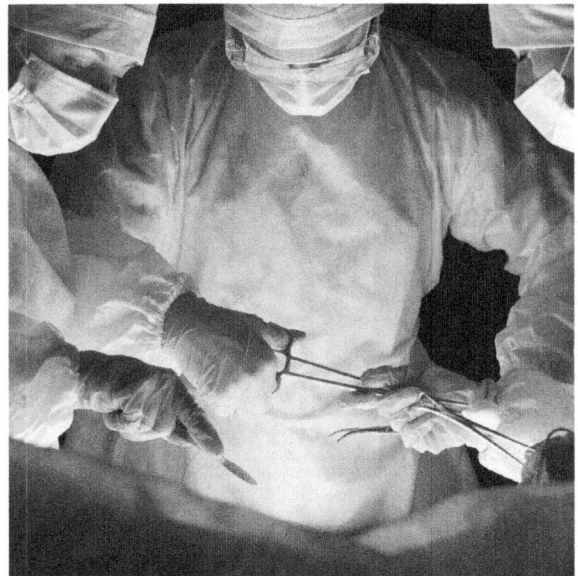

156.

157.

158.

159.

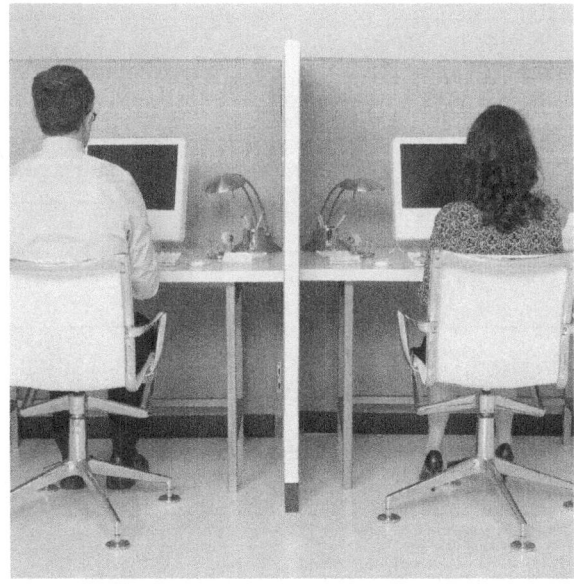

160.

161.

162.

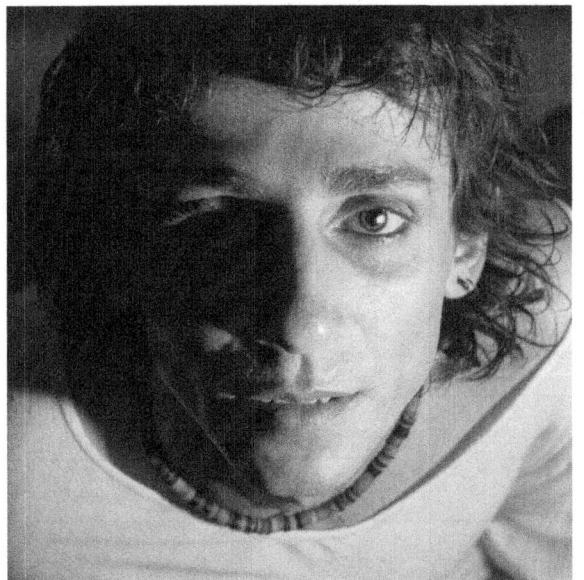

163.

164.

Avenue of the Baobabs, Madagascar

165.

166.

Havana, Cuba

167.

168.

169.

170.

171.

172.

173.

174.

175.

176.

177.

178.

Florence, Italy

181.

182.

183.

184.

185.

186.

187.

188.

189.

190.

191.

Florence, Italy

192.

103

193.

194.

195.

196.

197.

198.

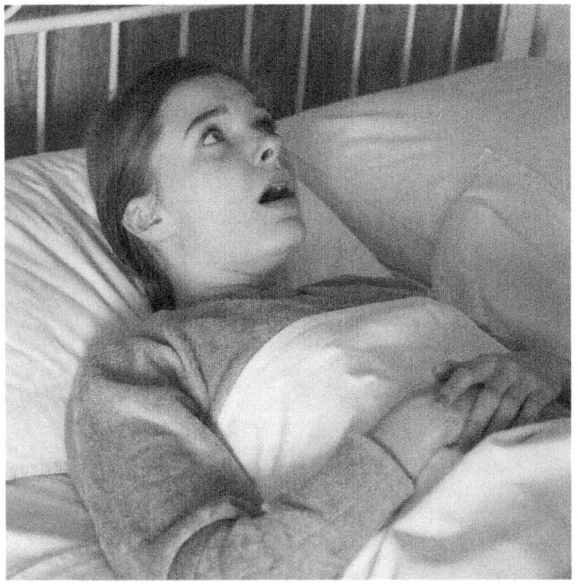

199.

200.

Istanbul, Turkey

201.

202.

Istanbul, Turkey

203.

204.

205.

206.

207.

San Francisco, California

208.

209.

Saint Basil's Cathedral, Moscow

210.

211.

Petra, Jordan

212.

213.

214.

215.

216.

217.

218.

Montevideo, Uruguay

219.

220.

Machu Picchu, Peru

221.

222.

223.

224.

225.

Buenos Aires, Argentina

226.

227.

228.

229.

Summer Palace, Beijing

230.

231.

232.

233.

Chefchaouen, Morocco

234.

235.

236.

237.

Seljalandsfoss, Iceland

238.

239.

240.

241.

Big Island, Hawaii

242.

243.

244.

245.

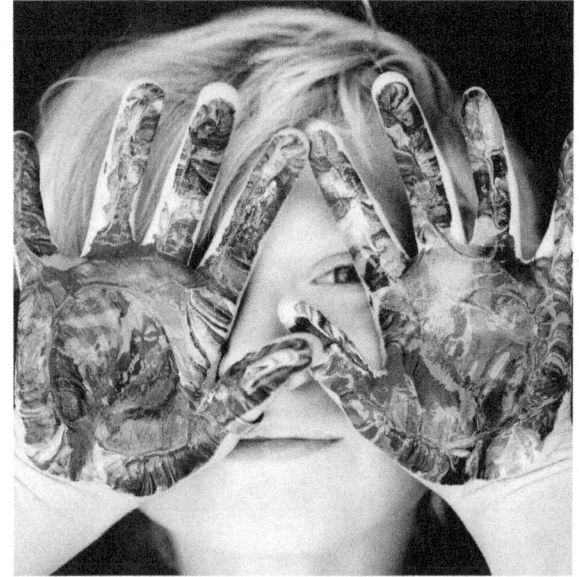

246.

Kyoto, Japan

247.

248.

249.

Mumbai, India

250.

251.

252.

253.

254.

255.

256.

257.

258.

Abbey of Fontenay, France

259.

260.

Neuschwanstein Castle, Germany

261.

....

....

....

....

....

....

....

....

....

....

....

262.

....

....

....

....

....

....

....

....

....

....

....

Neuschwanstein Castle, Germany

263.

Bukhansan, South Korea

264.

265.

266.

267.

268.

269.

270.

271.

272.

273.

274.

275.

Montmartre, Paris

276.

277.

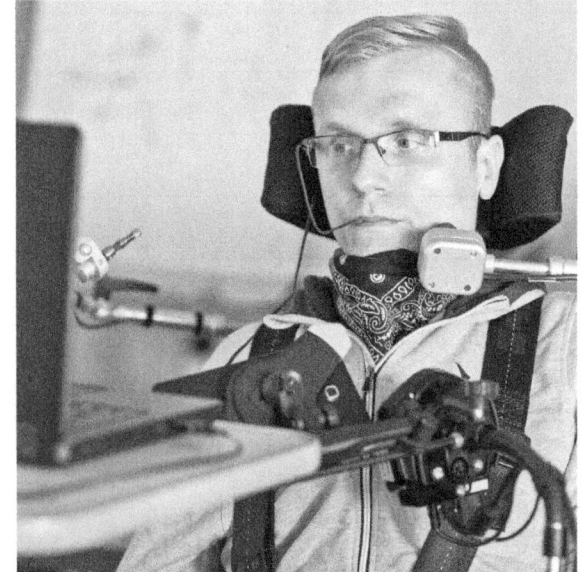

278.

Monument Valley, Arizona

279.

Ayutthaya, Thailand

280.

281.

282.

148

283.

284.

285.

286.

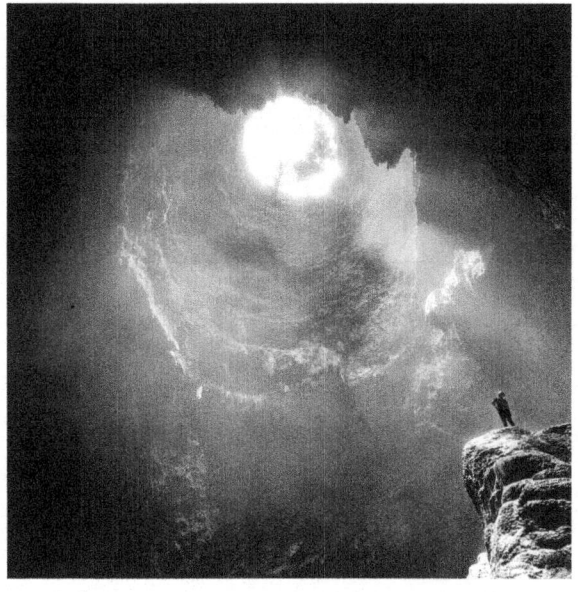

287.

288.

289.

290.

291.

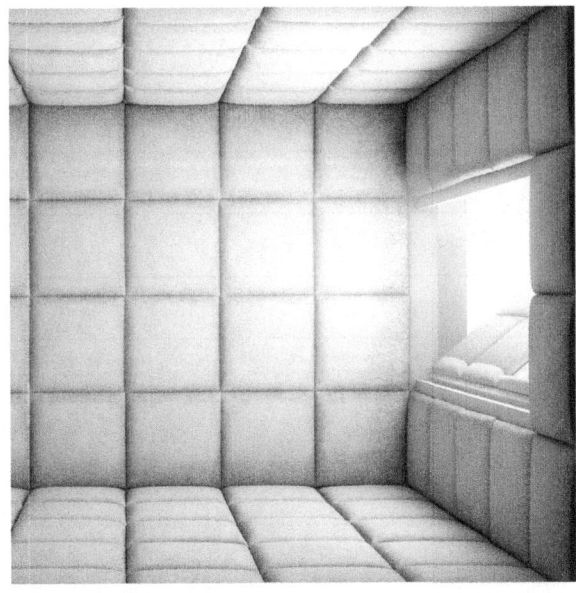

292.

293.

Arctic Sea

294.

Mù Cang Chải, Vietnam

295.

296.

297.

298.

299.

300.

301.
....
....
....
....
....
....
....
....

....
....
....
....

302.
....
....
....
....
....
....
....
....

....
....
....
....

303.

304.

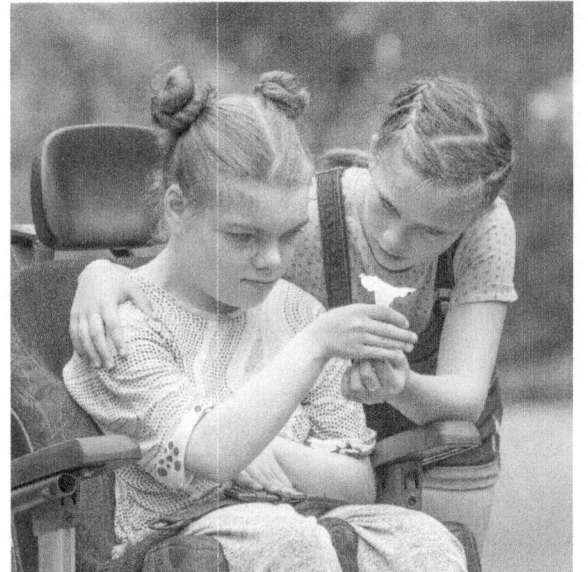

305.

306.

307.

308.

309.

310.

311.

312.

163

Supertree Grove, Singapore

313.

314.

315.

316.

317.

318.

319.

320.

321.

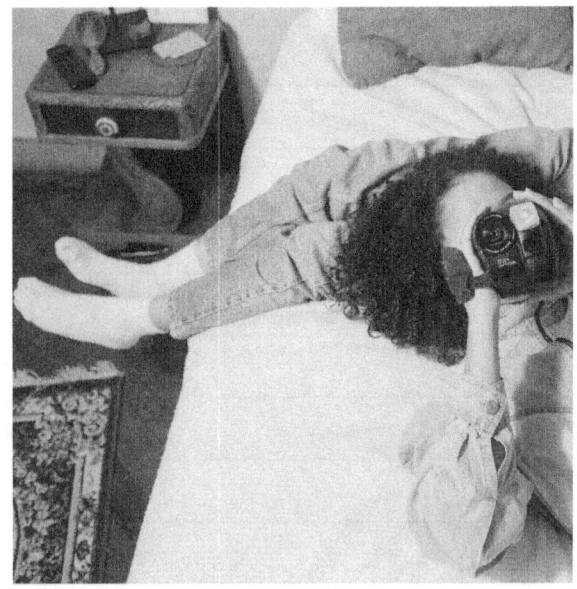

322.

323.

324.

325.

326.

327.

328.

329.

330.

172

331.

332.

333.

334.

335.

336.

337.

338.

339.

340.

341.

342.

343.

344.

345.

346.

347.

348.

Salvador, Brazil

349.

350.

351.
....
....
....
....
....
....
....
....
....
....
....

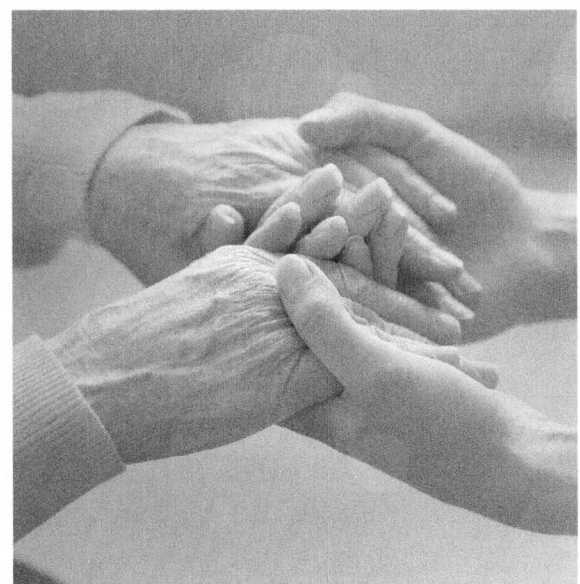

352.
....
....
....
....
....
....
....
....
....
....
....

353.

354.

184

355.

356.

357.

358.

359.

360.

361.

362.

Llanos de Cortez, Costa Rica

363.

364.

The Kimberley, Australia

365.

366.

Florence, Italy

367.
....
....
....
....
....
....
....
....

....
....
....

368.
....
....
....
....
....
....
....
....

....
....
....
....

Florence, Italy

369.

370.

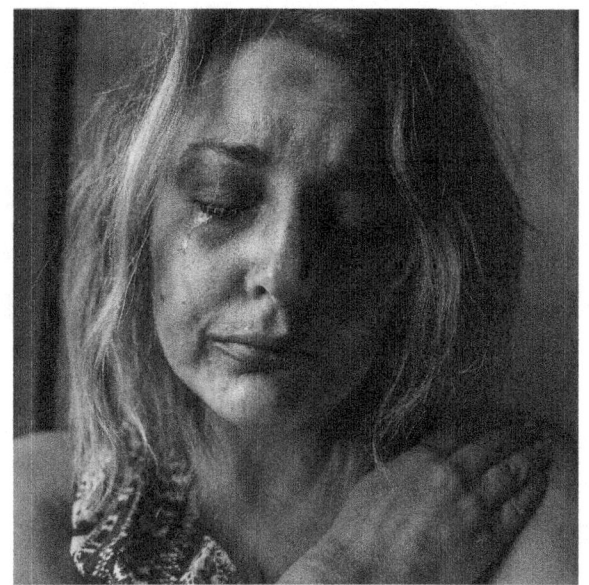

371.

372.

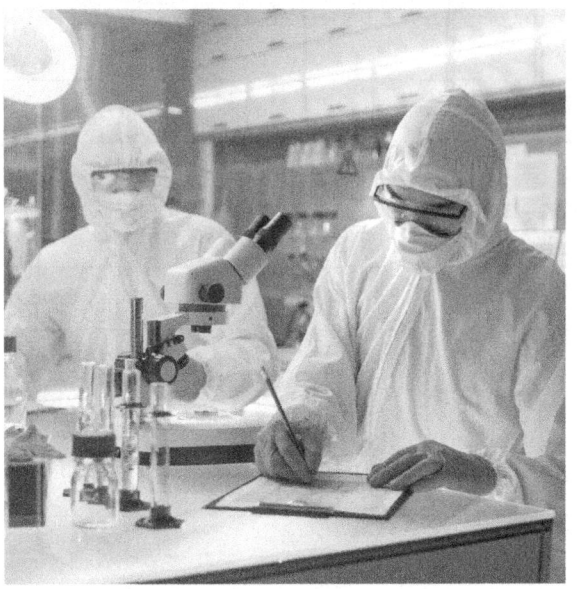

373.

374.

375.

376.

195

377.

378.

379.

380.

381.

382.

383.

384.

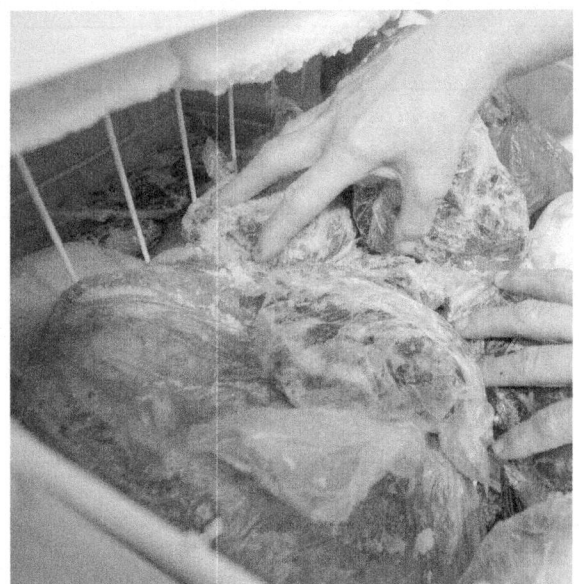

385.

386.

387.

388.

389.

390.

391.

392.

393.

394.

395.

396.

397.

398.

399.

400.

My New Life

Made in the USA
Monee, IL
19 December 2024

74507019R10125